Unidentified
Poetic Object

Unidentified

Poetic Object

Brian Henderson

Brick Books

Library and Archives Canada Cataloguing in Publication

Title: Unidentified poetic object / Brian Henderson.
Names: Henderson, Brian, 1948– author.
Description: Poems.
Identifiers: Canadiana (print) 20189067802 | Canadiana (ebook) 20189067810 | ISBN 9781771315005
   (softcover) | ISBN 9781771315029 (PDF) | ISBN 9781771315043 (EPUB)
Classification: LCC PS8565.E51 U55 2019 | DDC C811/.54—dc23

Copyright © Brian Henderson, 2019

We acknowledge the Canada Council for the Arts, the Government of Canada through the Canada Book Fund, and the Ontario Arts Council for their support of our publishing program.

The author photo was taken by Charlene Winger.
The book is set in Minion Pro.
The cover image is by Brian Henderson.
Design and layout by Marijke Friesen.
Printed and bound by Coach House Printing.

Brick Books
431 Boler Road, Box 20081
London, Ontario N6K 4G6

www.brickbooks.ca

For Charlene—
for her love, her compassion,
& her welcoming of the many varied lives of the world

Everything exists; even the things that don't.
—Ian Bogost

It is strange because we think language is a useful tool for referring to things—but when I open my mouth to talk about things, out comes another thing.

There is an object-like entity at the core of human being.
—Timothy Morton

…the infinite, the zero and the everyday…
—Marcus Boon

Between spirits and things, years pass.
—Walter Benjamin

Reading by Luciferin /

A whole field of sparks
How to be in the world suddenly
Surrounded
Yet another book left out
In the rainy accipiter glide silhouette
The words snagged on their own
Near night letters truck light tracers
These shooting star
Mimics instant lives of meteorites to be zipped
Off in those messages metaphors
Are tripwires for
The ghosts of things slivered silver
Wavy neuropeptides
Dispersed through dusk Perseids
Sight-trigger unencumbered
Words the known becoming
Smaller and smaller the
Blink of an eye and us
At the bottom of the field breathing
With moth-wing lungs

The Zombie Codex /

Wikipedia and the OED helpfully suggest zumbi fetish
In the Kikongo tongue zombi in a history
Of Brazil of 1819 by Robert Southey
Apparently there is slippery light
On every page that needs a reader to devour

What is ink but the knowledge of magic
Pulled through the hair of a corpse or maybe some other
pharmacology only the author is aware of

I am aware of being a newcomer to dramatic involution
Whose language might this be I am calling you from
That distant place

There is nothing mechanical about the dead
They have always been thinking through the pyre and the sky tree
thicket
And the box with its many pages its many wings and the shimmer
Of a word and the life slipping up through it
Is a zombie
Memory you refuse

Lightheadedness /

As in black seed shards under bird feeders sizzling
Into snow scattered type messages for Virgil or Dante or
Kurt Schwitters as in dizzy blonde as in Lady Luck as
In coming upon a line of reasoning so pure it
Intoxicates the afternoon as in drunk with mindlight everything
Speeded up each becoming its own energy only lighthouses light
Years as in what is the difference between a true
Fact and an imaginary one one hundred and thirty-three percent
Of Hannah Arendt's book written in English and the other
One hundred and thirty-three percent in another tongue or so
It would be in one of those true dreams we never understand as in
A moment of longing so intense I'm scooped out by love feather
Flame of scar that flickers up your belly oh I need more grace
Than I thought as in the solitary cricket winding its watch under
heat lightning flicker
As in the wind chimes warning of the place the two worlds
Collide with a sudden jangle
Clatter and things slip from the one world to the other
And possibly back again

Fizzed /

A raven bounces a call off the blue operculum
Of sky humbled by this and by Osterizers small
Eddies crushed glacial ice Spider Woman wind
Hounds brush fire stroke-enzymes if we keep going
We sense we are almost somewhere which keeps
Us going just when writing sidles up to the world
And pulls its plug forcing it to run on its backup
Generator and the words fizzed by vagrant
Voltage feel as if they are no longer
In their own language whichever one that might
Have been but from behind the door
That never opened they have the charm
And the secrecy of facts of evening light lifting dust
Like threshed time to a glowing haze

Cloud Lessons /

How to correctly modulate
Densities over great distances how
To dissipate and feather the edges
Of vanishing how to create a virga
Of memory that never lands but streams
Into a moment it colours without owning
How to qualify light carefully
With grief how to carry it in water
As colour how to trouble the grief
Of light with pattern how to pattern
Sound while giving it away how
To become empty how
To make the perfect soufflé
How to live in cross-currents
The ontology of crossing
A breathing that needs no breadth
How to understand the true nature
Of roofs the changing nature
Of maps and how the thing
Mapped under that pressure thereby reveals
Its plenitudes how to draw a flame
From wet ashes how to
Pray in ancient temples of water
The solubility of time the
Alphabet of lightning how to
Begin and how to end
How

The Rain Book /

The rain book is an early device for measuring the amount of
moisture in the atmosphere

Page curl describes a modest humidity spike in the early morning

Text bleed acknowledges the fragility of the attempt to fix
Memory and emphasizes writing's fluidity or perhaps

That the writer had suffered a recent or recurrent loss a kind of
winter a summer storm can render
A page illegible in a matter of minutes

But there is no such thing as a clean slate regardless of your desire ink
Is always the colour of water

And water is always the colour of something else

Is /

Is unfinished sky mud drift
Glacial karst meltwater
Writing some words in landscape shale creatures
Muskrat snapping turtle catbird cattail
Is trapline fishing camp axes fenceline musket barn railways
Silo highways power corridor aggregate extraction
Is neonicotinoid wind turbine drone surveillance extinctions
Just beyond this drumlin is small words along the Underground Railroad
Across reckless bodies of water in Anishinaabemowin
Whispered up from river stone field tarmac is another outwash with trees
And a sideroad at Irish Lake beyond that hillock
Is a coyote den at the rim of the aspen glade
Where a harrier ghosting finesses
Etymologies of sun-and-shadow shafted
Glide-beat-beat-glide fugue-words

Shadow Water Radio /

The radio in the flecked-by-turbine shadow flicker is squeezed
through a DNA torque gene driver the shimmering silence of the drive

Ravens fly off in all directions weaponed with gesturelight burning
off the scalded mercy of a stream

It sometimes seems you need to come a great distance to get to the
present

That body that appears as a pike is a verb in another language
Palatial thunder in the south

Under a bullet-riddled fuselage of night sky whatever happened
is still happening refractory in a catachresis of progress Proton
Station no longer a station dispersed settlement of Priceville not
likely
Founded by a Colonel Price the hacking treaties terra nullius

A thing inside a heading of thinking you're inside of
Falls the way a coin or a knife falls through still water

Turning waves of light lazily over over
Over and out

What Garden /

Perhaps I wasn't thinking but sleeping
How the narrative of things born out in often quite expensive
collisions is these houses we meet again and again history as an object
Lesson books whose words convert to sugar gunpowder ash
Or cosmetics occasionally fibre optics or electroshock
Your smile made of envelopes an ache which is
A syncope of the attic of the always receding garden behind the
house also
What is knowledge
See litter dream splices also what is faithful
See knowledge not what I thought
See love praxis the plural of its own soil because it imagines its
chicanery of lost opportunities
Each broken rhizome of which is replantable fire speaking in
beardtongue fireweed loosestrife dogbane Solomon's seal the tiny
golden bells of sweetgrass

Welcome /

And of those who have travelled there how many have come back stray light
Highlighting mistsilver with smudged saffron you could have walked into
That motionless horizonless mirror without either sky or water
If only a raft or dock or heron might have appeared
Osprey lofting a speckled torpedo or hemlock discover itself
Slivered in a sleet of current we don't hear even the slip of
Sleeve of silk-ripple over stone or
A single grouse from a long distance starting up its unstartable motor
The mirror opens a raft of sticks in your head where there's quite a range of curios
But they are unrelated to wherever you are

Soul Bodies /

Every soul is human but not at the same
Time it's only the bodies (oh those trajectories)
That differ the nonextant humans and
The extant nonhumans here is a bell at the apex of
Your dream despite what you thought

It's not made of darkness scattered
Rhapsody of quasi events through
Sky-clearing

Like someone wiping a blackboard clean

And there are the ghost lights

The who of things

Marks /

Within a steep or stretched charm
Slight variation circulates
Going underground at the sigil
Of the future aspen colonies
That can be thousands of years old
Though human-spanned trees but

Not quite so fast the end-all of each singularity

Burst catkin departure
Of a loved one as if
Clouds had knives you hurt
So solidly so be all
The open glances the
Lichen measuring
The north side of light where
The sound of a life stopping

Hides in its resistance open

Ash water tree nib
Pressure on paper leaves
The one anchor of want
Meaning wants so desperately

The Truth I Swear /

i.m. P.W.

The truth about arrows
The truth about personal
Armour the truth about love
The truth about hotel mattresses
Emitting the dreams of strangers
Into the software of your sleep
The truth about furniture generally
The truth about time
Rising out of the body
Like a volley of arrows
The truth about the alphabet
Rising out of the body
A museum of stolen objects
Whose organization is suspect
The truth about water
And its stony vocabulary
And about the GPS of language
And the choral works of wires
Truth of the truth
About the story about the frying pan
In which your mother struck your father
After he'd arrived home having been out
All night and your mother
Struck him over the head with the truth about stories
The truth about snow which in the sun
Is silverware showing off
Or a dream of death the truth

About the book of junk being
About decollecting the truth
About string and string theory strung
Together with its other universes
Right to the brink of this string
About not going on and going on still

House Made of Doors /

Pain is a house you build your self a name with a small mirror at first
There is diversification and there is conformity one evening
A sunset like a blast furnace and its rivers of ore and slag no one's
looking at the other side of the sky
Where things are coming up infinitely far away doors like mobiles
swinging open and closed glinting a house made of doors flying
Off their hinges

Swifts switchblading the last light

Whatever night is made of you gather up

The dream you're trying to remember something for

There is not a willow with memories knotted in it
There is not a battle worth remembering
Not a hem of time rickracked with stars
Not not nothing and the fullness of nothing
With exits and entrances
Patient in the dark

Dictionary of Overlapping Things /

Thoughts like trains departing
At various times and the previously
Departed can sometimes be
Overtaken by the just-now thought and vice
Versa given variations in speed such
That collisions occur or correlations
Align through the wave medium
Into what people often call a life
That depends so much on where or
What time in the evening these events
Might even be noticed if
You are watching TV or
Redefining the word schedule
In your dictionary of overlapping things
Which has been one of my weaknesses
Small harmonic distortions in the refraction
Station's propagation or a Kirlian photograph
A timetable for it that might even now be combustible
And with which we may soon coincide

Intensification Effect Produced by Deformations /

Skunk dragging her lab of spoiled alchemy down the ravine at moonrise

Someone standing alone in a field with shoes of fire

Breathe says the doctor the swim coach the yogini

Breath shaped by what gives itself to us

Breath like time extending in every possible direction

And at the shore of things blown by moonlight the spray of shadow

That dreaming sound who is the one beside you

The sound of the ghost of the moon pulling the tractor out of the ditch

Trees for Instance /

You can only begin to imagine
How many lives are liquid here flowing
Up through the vowels of your bones
Consonantal drift red shifting everyone you've
Seen or touched who's seen or touched you still
Filamentous myceliafy into the chromosomes of
Seas the colour of the opposite of dying
Inventing a whole person with hidden sugars
In a hardwood forest
Nourishing offspring with fungal root networks
Liquid until the light comes down for them

I am as lucky as a tree diagram a map of moving water
I am a tiny chemical of unknowing
Draw me out of your hunger I am dreaming somewhere the
susurration of aspen leaves

I stand in the inbuilt house of sunlight
Filled with the internal desire machines
Of names or the afterlife of names

And in the fall we walk through the histories
We know without having to read

Ravens Carry on their Research into Human Thinking /

Scorched wheat coffee ink from maple bark
Ink spilled on a pillow
Pillow of sky on which people imagine us glyph-written ha

They imagine the moon struck by a stream of black darts
But it's just us one at a time flying through
And even though they've hidden everything they can
That light burns a few ideas to cinders

If they hear the knocking and whispering the cadence of black
holes across light years rippling in their skulls they don't let on

The politicians bankers CEOs corporate environmentalists
convene cracking jokes
But we'll really get them going by sleeping with their money

If they thought of all distances as material they'd always be here
But instead we begin to find all these evacuations
Imagining everything but always coming back only to themselves

What happens if we replace distance with dubious spindles or
waved goblets left-handed jewel boxes
Would there be a key of lightning

What if we give them back the ball we lent Veronique through
which she knew the passing world from the train
Which life would be lived
Which switch would be thrown and how far

We'll take the words out of their dictionaries
Smear honey on their triggers in a series of controlled police
experiments
Fill the observation towers of their clocks with smoke
In a room with two humans whose sexes have been removed
We'll add a third filled with longing who speaks a different language

In the sheen of our occasional mourning we grieve for them their lost
Opportunities everything they turn their backs on are
programmed to forget
And after which they name policies or prisons or political parties

The One about the Nongivenness of Things /
How to Master the Rotary Phone

Everything seemed fine until a minute ago a small fragment
Of one of your memories seems to have slivered
Itself into my skin oh that's not you everyone
Seems to be speaking another language politics
Misrepresenting its own truth laundering kakopoliteia
Dog-whistle half-life squid ink black snake root
Lighting up the half-lit light shade a moment of perpetuity as
Different from eternity assuming of course we
Could agree on definitions the awkward grace
Of vultures dialling in their dihedrals the sky
With its many coloured ribbons where clouds effortlessly
Age let's agree at least there are moments of
Suspension shrunk nearly to human
Comprehension idiogrammic centrifuge contact
Cement Hudson eight one four eight four
The Cisco Kid the interpretation of breathing redside
Dace where each thing can open the wildernessing
And if not shouldn't there be

Bodies Falling past Time /

The Aztecs believed you thought with your heart and who's to say otherwise

I came out of the bedroom this morning to the semaphoring of the sun through dark snow clouds

I brought all my years with me each one weightless as a word

Not that I'm counting but I pretty much have a dictionary

But no not in that language

The sun slides off the balcony into the cedars

What should I have said

Proof is something we leave to alcohol

In the dream the Luger that became my father's in the war Jammed when the hounds coloured like killer whales bounded past and the agents attempted to force an entrance

Agents of what

There are secrets lying around everywhere at the hour of this writing at the hour of death at the hour of birth now asleep under a sutra of snow

Perhaps no time has passed since then

Only me

Sliding like a kind of talking ghost past the holding-still
Myriads the sticky objects the billowed plastic bags the icari the still
Possible syntax Nezahualcoyotl Ereshkigal
Deportation edicts the safe houses the email the glances the
caresses the archery lessons of Upper Paradise Road
In fact the complete works of time

Machine for Inquiring into the Nature of Singularities /

First the path thinks the thinking of coyotes out loud and their
delight in fermented apples

A least weasel with its black-tipped tail and its thirst for blood the
matted head of a snowshoe hare still white in the ruddy dogwood
glistening

And then a couple of humans in winter jackets per-
haps preoccupied with the distractions of themselves

Along the way trees bare and spangled with the first freezing rain

A few small apples turned russet and silver marking cycles of
freeze and thaw remain moored by lines of glass to their old lives

Goblin faces beaks and ears of bleached and weathered vertebrae
winking with menace amongst glazed glacial rock

And when they ask for proof of existence
What do we do we slap our pockets
Looking for papers as if trying to keep warm

And glance back to the hill over which we think we've just come

And look at our empty hands the air crashing into them

Vacuum Glass History /

In which stand trees every twig of every branch of which is a vacuum tube glistening
With a music of creaking and clattering collected from across the universe

Imagine dropping a drawer of knives

Why do we think we know where we are

Imagine a Buddha thinking each idea falling through the mind or rising crackling as in the ten thousand
Volts of a Jacob's Ladder in its spindle neuron sleeve of glass

Faint hurt crossing the impermeable barrier into this place of the flying skeletons
Bones glittering like galaxies on the long wave
Where water moves infinitely slowly prismatic smeared
Resonance drawn right out of the atmosphere the other side
Of history the remains of the never-seen glistening that nearly blinds storm of sunlight bearing down

Excommunicados /

Having given up their voices stars
Let them fall to earth as the
Ratcheting clatter of wood frogs spring peepers ringing out their
Brightness in the otherwise stillness and what might appear
Darkness to us

That was the night of the day in April
You were nearly killed at the crossroads after all the undeveloped
unlikely undistributed elements arriving at that still journey
Arrived

You standing miraculously there alone in the empty field blue
and empty
Blue and empty sky road strewn with hard debris shiny and
broken things lazy flashing red yellow red yellow

As if there were parallel worlds
Or the threat of substitutions across impermeable borders a
camera trailing its images under a field
Of rogue stars river
Of forgetting weather irises
Blue
Yellow

Light /

One investigation revealed light's origin as bone but another proved
Aspirin a third found evidence for the tongues
Of meadow larks and another the waterfall
Someone even thought the word of a god just before
Shadows began to dig their own graves

But after the fire tore you
After the fireball of exploding gas that wanted to make a rocket of you
Inquisition of fire

Standing in that light's wounding
A film drenched in the cruel exposure of pain
Glass wave the body is the true ghost

Phantasm spool spun out by spindles of
Incombustible light light made of bad luck and of ash
Light made of shadow and light made of water
Light made of fireflies and blindness
Of broken valves
Each one inventing their own
Allowing us to see

And of that brightness you can't be emptied

Zeno's Attractor /

When you pluck it out of the river with a name
And heave it against the wall it
Unfolds ripples suddenly slowing elongates
Arriving at the wall always unfolding slowing
Where there is no wall on the wall
Is a brush with death and how
Time flies out of it just there

User's Manual /

Part A / How to make a surveillance mask

Really you can't begin
To understand anything by reading it
To loved ones especially here unless
We can finally take a step
Back and begin to think of wondering
As setting up a diffraction
Pattern such that some things
In the landscape become
Visible while others take a back seat
And what we see depends wholly
On the edge clusters of the words
We use in that country
Where there is no communication
Possibly only surveillance each one
Has a mask or helmet made
From tin and leather wicker or some
Braided material with an aerial
From which a small piece of coloured
Cloth distends but if you close the trap
Door in time with the small telescope gear
Their sinister quality begins
To fade and you can descend
The stairs when the library has books no longer
And press this button you may have to press
More than once but whatever you do don't
Take it out of the box

Part B / How to think like water

Begin purling around things piling things
Up against other things carrying things
For varying distances do not breathe
On the fine instigations of tides or their
Formulae minions empty one
Tiny glossary at a time once
The fuel is shut off you must rely
On love which first you must define or fail
To believe in to know
You have so many things in your envelope
Try one of them now

Part C / How to read to loved ones

Part C is presently unavailable please
Look under the song you just passed with
Its eddy its medallion of nostalgia relief
Or diplomacy once you decide which return
To the definition of love under surveillance or
Under water depending on what hours have been
Gleaned or in which vehicle you find yourself
Weeping the first authorization oriole
And apply the polyploidy signal
Continually with slow motion wing-
Beats of cloudburst tepal glaciations
Until it opens on a lake or large bay that nearly seems
Likely under three steadily illumined

Orange lights falling supine into the bardos
Of the real things you've had to spread out
There where their reflections now appear

Mereology /

Meerkats the study of meerkats
Or mirages possibly
Places of perfect thirst
Even though the language is

And even though the language is not

Even though the language is not mine to carry
Matter is dreamlike

Dreamlike and the rest performative continuous
Continuous streamers really

Born from the I don't know what
The continuous I don't know

So it's good to know something
No matter how particular

The broken elm outdistancing the disease for decades
Answering the stanzas of rain and sun sun and rain
With leaves lichen insects with birdsong birdsong and inevitably
Fungal explosions

We speak across distances

Across distances that are feral so close together
From river to flowing and back
From tree to phloem and back
From mockingbird to its vast library of songs and back
From Mir to the South Atlantic Anomaly and deorbit
The longing of Meera Bai for her Mountain Lifter and back

Distances begun
With the study of the parts of mirrors
The study of the barely-thereness of things
Each a word holding open a world

Unfolding /

Tonight great seas of wind crash over the house
The ship yaws and pitches the fog in my mind the last few days
blows out like a torn genny
Luckily there's an anchor
The house moans

It's been a difficult year

You're in the spare room with a cough and I'm thinking about the nights you'll be in town

Your skin bends light things orbit around you
You attract stray thoughts and the thoughts are mine

When I splash down in you now it's a staged firework that hangs in the sky

Your eyes are the silver-blue they must always have been

Just because it's random the virtual doesn't offer free will
Choice is a category of instinct
In the realm of choice we are the chosen

One good answer I've found is yes

Oh look here's this picture
From Dante's View with you in the clouds and Death Valley six thousand feet below floored with rivers and pools
The fires of hell quenched with last night's monsoons

Your bemused smile

Unfold a second in or near the present
And time flows out in all directions
Unfold one life
And there is another's

Words /

Everything swims upstream against the stickiness of vision
The street the house in the street the room in the house
The desk in the room the book on the desk at which I'm sitting
The cut forest the various chemistries the words in the book
everything
Is a door including the thumping
Helicopter of the grouse its wings pounding like a heart
You've stuck to my vision in the kitchen like the persistent
Brightness that remains once you close your eyes on the window's
Gathering of the morning you don't hear the helicopter you
Hear a motor splutter one thing is always more than
One thing don't you find words for instance a word is
A door a sound an etymology that is to say a continual
Transformation in time a reach is unique but also
Reusable for instance the word I'm thinking of bitcoin
Telepathy autoimmunity chrysalis Lily Cup landfill
Tom-tom aubade ocean otter operand is probably being
Used in someone else's sentence right now is a series
Of syllables or a single letter letter not yet mailed you
Put it in one fire and it burns green in another blue in
Another orange in another it's knowledge that burns
To cinders when known and so forth in a secret
Solution and its invisibility rises to the surface and
Floats away though it's addressed to you and you
Have to drink the solution that might be
Purple or teal or tea-coloured and has
A pleasantly sweet smoky finish

Collection / How to Bend Time with a Flashlight in Your Own Home

Bright with the shadows flung out from them
Each one of these instances is where you
Had once been and though they seemed
Finished then each continues to emit
Its separate times that intermesh in
The interference pattern known as the
Hologram of the broken chairs something
At last possible like a flashlight or a bottle
Cap with an inscription that reads
Unopen me fine each thing is wild
With its omniscient narrator its
Politician who says trust me its
Pretended exterior its proliferation
The likelihood of sitting down
And sorting things out finally debris-omancy
Of a life in the horse latitudes jetsamology
And in the pulchritudes laganology
Shiny shards of mirror destined for the
Museum of letters so many of which have
Fallen out of use and hence we no longer
Recognize them as such how many things
We once were able to say how many
Different evenings come to think of it
Time is a prism all it does is bend
Light to different degrees even
The holograph of rain on the river

Unidentified Poetic Object /

after Nicholas Thoburn, Anti-Book

Brain wing light
Secret fume box medicine
Future history stain scan
Pyrotechnical blowgun flight shadow seam
The body eroded not by time but by the incessant downpour of
dream objects

Life is almost excusable because it has no teleology or telephone

Thinking far out to sea amid the archipelagoes of plastic
The whatnot swept out into its waiting arms
Some will tell you happiness is a long sleep with a pistol under
your pillow
But it doesn't matter what's under your pillow
You are naked regardless

And the sea will unplug its currents
Putting an end to what people call climate

Imagine the beauty of such stasis the collapsed
Battlefronts the hydro-oneiric gravity waves

You won't need a phone to hear for miles in the underground caverns
where muons wink like missed opportunities

Pallasite /

Like a small chunk of space-rock fluid totemics of crystallography the mind
Could careen down into the sea of some distant earth and splash out
Or like a small bird flutter off into the noise underbrush and be hidden with its small dredges of light

You knock at the door and the one who answers wants something from you

In every drawer there are patterns that match the night sky at various times of the year

Pine siskins know something about that light which they hide in their wings to splash fanned out gold fluid and burnt off weightless
Just over there

Flashbang mortar of a grouse in a thicket

Meanwhile the mind with its punished metal door hinged to the waste electronics bin not far from the river lies open listening for the liquid olivine buzz of the vanished life of a nighthawk on some earthlike planet

The Book of the River of Silver /

You could stand here and be blinded at night you could
inadvertently drown
Some people do not know what they are feeling tiny
topographies could be revealed by melting old coins along the
lines of your thinking

A pooling could be above or below sea level

A pool can be weighed but not seen into the wind however might
mention your name or the name of someone close to you or a
rapids might

Is there a skin of ice
Is there a forest or a meadow beside the river

Even so it is only a clock
It might take an image of you downstream and throw it in the
lake but more likely just bend it and scatter it into the heated air

It might have been acceptance acknowledging sorrow

It might've been a kingfisher or a larch for all you know if you
ever could
You can't any longer buy anything with it but you could
Photograph it or give it away

It is harder to write with silver than with ink

In the Field /

Burst phantasms Catherine wheel seed heads rinsed with tiny chemical washes of
Feeling the field is an organ of sensation practice beginning again from a different direction
Not that this would render things less perplexing even if it could be done

I don't want to be beheaded for predicting the future to be found to be harbouring mice tiny soldiers of
Satan the accountability apparatus
Is restless a bardo of failed
Reverse-engineered justice looking for victims

There's shooting throughout the counties of blame
Through the fine air of dusk
Its colours collapsing through the risen dust
Of hunters killers soldiers cops of drones of IEDs
With whom am I struggling?

A field returning to forest senses the extent of continuous darkness and awakens with phytochromes

What if each word were a tiny conflagration of letters of touch that could change genetic makeup what if it memorized photosynthesis and timed feeling with sunlight what if it were a bowl that could hold a life a river who could flood it gifts from crows bottle cap foam dart marble Donald Duck Pez dispenser orange glass shard

What if each word were a not-word a wilderness word

A difference
Between before and after action potentials in the kettle field
across which coyotes stare at me in stillness

After a Long Walk with Ravens /

A barking cat tumbler
Turning a snoring chainsaw a tocking clock
Dialling from the 1950s listen closely the ravens say
In many languages some inaudible in the treetops
For these secrets you will now be carrying
They are knocking on your skin with weightlessness

I was out walking by the wetland
I was in the kitchen

Looking out the window at night across English Bay to
mountains
In Grey Highlands I was
In our bed smelling your skin I
Was walking back to the field of the wasps' nest that later was
becoming a subdivision I was walking by the river
You can walk a long time

Many have been shot walking
Or standing or sitting or sleeping

And if you were to keep on walking anyway
At what point would time fall in love with you
And would it be because it can't read the secrets or knows them
already

Interregnum of Extractions /

So we've burned all the bridges
And now find fording streams difficult
We've stood at the edge
Of the unspoken but heard it merely as failed conversation
Or fireworks

So easy does it can we hit a circle
Four inches square in nonlocality
Can we draw out the small poisons from each other
At distances of a few meters

A series of risky events unheard of a few decades ago
That each participant could only foresee under extreme duress

These toils don't hear us any longer but disperse
Across taigas of extraction at latitudes we scarcely know

The last latitude to pass through us completely
Was the infinite river in which each
Hydrocarbon bore the memories of the persons
Through whom it had passed before arriving at
The demolished bridges the broken
Stone cascade pillows undercut wing dams
Whirlpool deposition and erosion braid
Of us

Small Device for Removing Phenomena from the Future /

Made of silicate spokes crossing
Silver's fissures' wavering
Woven emergency it turns out
Turning out from you like a blink
No longer hesitant bleeding synaptic
Ohms but engendering a field of purposeful strikes
One thing after another leaving
The mind with its vandal etymology leaving
It behind on a string of copper and gold
Retrieved from antique electronics and
Its map of where not to go because
Sequence is another unreliable narrator
We put too much trust in before we go out
Dazzled scattered across
The network a raven a refrigerator
Wind in cedar elm or ash take a
Mirror for instance on one side
Is the present and on the other
The past and on the other the future
Endlessly accumulated and this
Is called going forward

Apantomancy /

The partially burned evidence the foresight
Strategy of bone sovereignties
Of dust and plastic iron filings of tin pop
Can museums of riverine sandbars on
The concessions matryoshka dolls of your
Address as a child in this house
In this street in this town in this
Country in this universe a node in this
N+1 series that people used to call
Time comparing the distances
A signal travels the signal
Of your name rippling out in the light
Cone until it strikes something called
A table or someone's ear the
Heartwood in a table or someone's
Tongue or Thorazine entropies
Of law or pneumonia black holes
Of the forgotten bending us
Around their invisibility
Without an opening intricately
Open debris books once known
As dictionaries scrying books
Called poetry by people once

Varves / How to Repair an Atomic Clock with Graptolites

We arrive at one place only it's always another
Then someone thinks it might be possible
To have a conjugation of the one that's closer than it appears
Seismic-ed waiting
For time to precipitate out
No matter the excuses no one had been
I think interrogated but Manitoulin cobble beaches
Silurian crinoids and corals no one
Is certain where this is leading the wrack
Of shales and dolomites aside we've always been
Told a single line through time is best or
Maybe fastest but I have my doubts overexposed
By the floating chill river of fog an ambush
To return to a previous moment might be
Someone's idea of a joke the book of poems
Left out in the thunderstorm overnight becomes
What after the deluge fossilized
Nautiloids eurypterids as Baltica crashes
Into North America south of the equator speed is indeed
Duration even if instantly
What does duration mean anyhow
When it is infinitely divisible
Without getting smaller as you walk
Toward her camera in very long
Exposure exfoliating a stream of memories
I can take comfort in the fact that shallow sea
Won't want those shells those word
Casings those open secrets back anyway
Or will it

The Visitors /

Anyway something much more significant is how things fall
towards you when you least expect it gravity for instance
A cause of many errors and celebrations such as the white bench
landed among the Scotch pines listening
With their needles to the conversations of absent visitors or a lilac
alone in a meadow who on closer inspection has the company of
many almost once-ordered stones
Among whom a tarnished brooch with wings a perfectly intact
teal bottle of Davis' Vegetable Painkiller an iron leg-hold trap
whose language is rust rather than blood a dried-up well with a
boulder thrust in its throat

You have to ask who are the visitors here when the last time
you woke remembering a dream was what's with the speech of
thunder substitutions and if so for what it could be significant for
the plot or the burnt-out subjunctives of displacement

The Incommensurate /

Though incommensurate with itself language nonetheless
Somehow shoots a few arrows into the vanishing point of things
which have come here from a great distance
Which makes it clear we have come here from a great distance or
are asleep
To the future or for example the untenable proposition of flight
from hollow bones
On second thought let's assume music streams through feathers
from a great distance
Let's assume love is the name of the ten-thousand-year-old spear
point found in 1970 not far from where I live with my wife in a
house built for someone else in 1997 on glacial outwash that tried
on the disguise of a farm in 1854
Let's manage our assumptions from a great distance and
understand distance is timing leaving us beside ourselves
sometimes even with laughter or maybe a wound made of
porcupine quills or with longitude because the ink with which
it's written is time-sensitive and there is no such thing as the
opposite of meaning

How to Survive a Decomposition Event /

1) Listen to everything

We are looking for that which permeates
Everything and of which everything
Partakes given that neutrinos charm-type quarks
Tachyon mirrors have already
Been invented that is discovered we are
On the verge of a decomposition event
And if so why don't they just appear rather
Than fraternizing with the invisible where
Is thy sting someone must have left
In a drawer it's true we have no real
Way of organizing the place only letters
Patent the wind puts its mouth to
The instrument of your body and blows
You make the most gorgeous sounds

2) Welcome the bodhisattvas

Welcome bodhisattvas of the sunlight
Flushed shadow of lost flicker flight over
The meadow where we're lying
To ourselves and everyone else which
We accept with the equanimity of
Photosynthesis or its paroxysm village
Within the gigantic industrial
Wind-factory-without-workers

That has its roofs blown off every evening
Just before sunset wouldn't a cocktail go
Well now to think the unknown
As depth is to profoundly underestimate
Surfaces each word imagines
Its heaven once its work is done here maybe
We're inventing tiny machines
To harness the slippery energy of such starlight

House /

They listen inside to intermittent radio
Broadcasts in the forties or watch
Episodes of Maverick or Danger Man with a
Christmas tree beside them in the house
Without doors the weather is their silence
The diaspora of words a longing a long way
Away how is it they bind to the heart
In the centre don't say they're wanting
To leave or to enter the house
Floats on its currents one generator
For every hope such a house hoards
Its memories and forgets they are gone
Such a house is a god with a cellar
It sees and even at night calls
To the passage of light in its darkness
It has a name for you that misses you
But only slightly because time displaces
Its stairs can never be your stairs the house
Might yet harbour hostility yet can it
Ever be finished collecting even though
I am inside I can never enter

Cloud Encounter Box with Flow-Through Lungs /

Not being from around here every waking moment
Has not stopped me from not trying to open the little box on the counter
Clockwise from a pang at the edge of a hinge
Is a shadow of air I am standing in
Clockwise from the clouds unfamiliar as pyrodictium
Stella haloarcula I am standing in
A burst of starlings what I think is
A waking moment but mentioning that could be a mistake

Let me start again
What do you mean by around here
And by counterstarlings
At any rate I can't open it because it's locked
Which is a mistake
Everything has a home but not in the human mind
I trip and fall like rain through the counterclouds
We'll have to start again

Counterclockwise means the wisdom of the other clock
The one with its time stored in an inaccessible box
A self who's nearly not there here in the dark
Waiting for things to start again
Not realizing they already have

Contraband /

Each time we cross the likelihood of a return
Becomes more remote though we might know
The ways of crossing intimately

As when your breathing
Is the sound of a little soft motor
On the other side of the night
Villages in a dream

Maybe interiority is the outskirts
Where love would have been

A fisher on the outskirts the flightpurr
Of a chickadee or a motionless snowshoe hare
Vistas into leaf-emptied hardwoods

Things become sharper with distance except
Memory which becomes oblivion or dolomite
But the things remembered are ablaze

Somehow each box has a box and each box a key and each key
And so forth even if truth doesn't recognize us at the borders of
longing
Lost papers hidden soft gamma repeaters

I should take up rereading

What I know dims
What I don't shimmers what I don't have
Is weightless
What I do
Weightless

Swifts spend more than all of their lives in the air
Where a fire can be built out of anything
Even all the mistakes of a lifetime

Tangut Cloud Crumhorn /

The mind a go-between music of multiple contagions

As if the whole forest had come into the room in a thunderstorm

Or a desert its dunes swept waves over the black city in 1380

And two hundred years later the language evaporated like the water in the city before it

And on the verge of the dunes a verdant plain with horses a tent with prayer flags

That's how it was in every room the accumulating vectors of landscapes

Each room shaped by the weather in it each instrument by the sound it makes

Each life with its handful of candles

Its match of cardiac impatience

City /

Maybe we're done fooling
Around with politics and the inevitable
Misplacements of irony and poison
Shouldn't we know for our own good
Who's trying to kill us or turn us into money but
The roundabouts are endless maybe silkiness
Has a god of sex and your snappy answers
Just want someone to believe in them for two nights
The city of Rome lay at our feet hazy antique modern
Afoul of history and its many disruptions replacements
Re-enactments you wouldn't want the children to
Actually be able to read these stones these
Cars these expensive scandals these
Illusions of mastery twenty-five foot
Yucca trees but that's not Rome that's
Sorrento the windswept pines
You mustn't hesitate to subpoena who knows
What they might say now
Look at Rimbaud who was not
Interested in beauty and so left poetry early
Small ashen windows
Take on light meanwhile
In Firenze Dante's friend Cavalcanti
Didn't sail off in a paradiso either
And in Praiano grazi-ay is how they say it

Imaginary Berlin /

1) In the library of angels Schreibtischtäter of near compassion or possibly spies

Because impatience has broken off bits of me
And I'm not whole
Beginning with small accidents and going on from there
Silently driving spending the night driving
To reach the ocean at sunrise in the mirror
The books are deeper than water
I didn't know what I wanted and I couldn't wake up
So why should I be spared
The manuscript
Has yet to be deciphered
And all this time I have been forgetting
In the cosmological section there are cosmetics
In the biological section transporting fluids and in the recipe section stars
But what does it say
You could be composed
In encrypted tendril language
Or maybe not

2) Lost quires

Inexplicably there are thousands of solutions
None of which is convincing
It is snowing outside in black and white

You could buy hypnogogia over the counter then
But naps were expensive
I'm learning to take photographs of the photographs in my dreams
Not that there are that many
But those few are of a future that has had no past
In them there is often singing but everything else is folded
When life breaks in
You are floating on the calyxes the mouths of vases the green river the rainbows of pipes
There is nothing but windows
Chopping up the field of vision
How can anyone see into the present
Or is that what the present is

3) Nothing after 1950 can be carbon-dated

The particles are dispersed too thoroughly in a network of rosettes or ziggurat jars
How many times might you have changed your life since then
And what about the code word Bsafe how
Can we complete that at the checkpoint when
The storyteller is a wanderer in the landscape of language

It's where thinking is perpendicular to things that I get lost
All those women in their cloudbursts wet with secret knowledge
What is our ratio anyway of carbon to writing of water to dream
Whatever it is it's not what you think

Wait scrap that
Some moment of truth recedes as if it could have been grasped
But by then it will have been snowing for forty days and forty nights
All my unconsciously abandoned futures

4) Like the Codex Seraphinianus

First the outline was drawn then the text flowed
Around the flowerets and fruits the wall that was soon to come down
Was the author the scribe was the after the before
Was the thinker the doer who loaned me his jacket
Nonetheless the ongoing reminiscences

Some of these herbs are unknown
Trees with their little chimneys of flame radical extraction machines
The snake with a hound's head the scissor bush the photon bugs
I'm thinking out loud in a language no one understands I'm
practicing
Listening to the voices of things I step out onto the balcony of
Wearing impatience on my sleeve
I need to do something about that before the sun sets completely
It's also possible the page has been copied from a well-prepared draft
But life is usually not like that

5) All this is difficult to prove as long as we're unable to read the text

Picayune perhaps but the line is a functional entity in the Hidden Markov Model
Where there are more possibilities than just meaningful or meaningless
And where the curve floats and refuses to flatline as if you were sitting atop the tallest tower
Willkommen im Paradies

If you have the gallows glyphs you need only add a plume vertically
There or there but here they just look and behave like words
Shimmering in their fragility there in the forest

They have the interiors of tiny creatures hearts spleens enigmas
The women holding their stars pretend not to see them floating by
In the lives of others even in the lives of enemies with whom I'm so complicit

Couldn't I just imagine something more likeably interventionist
Why is the mystery always stalled at someone's actions rather than their mere being here

6) How many dreams can you be having at once

That's funny I was just thinking that
And this is a plus
The wind dropping its exaggerated dramas
So I can hear the softer ones unravelling inside the house
Its Ghibelline parapet and secret room under the porch
Where we dismantled as kids the machinery of the blossoms the aliens left behind
And I realized it's not the Escher hand
But the skeletal hand in the Seraphini box
That writes the manuscript
And when I came out it was a different house
Control alt manuscript the one where you need a selfie
Which of course is none of the above
And don't pretend you don't know what I'm talking about
You can triangulate anything with nothing and plot where you are
But really here cannot determine anything
Where after all are your homing glasses after the explosions
The ghosts of snow fly up spiralling in their bone dust
I pack a suitcase with an Easy-Bake Oven a penknife
an Underwood Leader all the patience I can find
And hope for the best
But that's not something
I would have said

7) Heights

Anyways always stand at the edge
Never leap or step back

There's something worth thinking about here
But it's not here

If you leap you pour through a scene like mercury
The filmmaker can't keep up with you
Only your life is not a film

Let the record show we have no idea who the author might be
Let alone the scribe or scribes or the persons who applied the
colours so pathetically
And what is that stupid music

Depression is a very heavy knife
But we're not talking about that

There is so much we are not talking about
The door through which we gesticulate for instance
The bzzt bzzt of the short-circuit in the soul the hazmat suits
Or the chemistry of inks words used to drink
However on waking I'll be going to the library

These are not light-years but mere days
And even though time is reversible
Nothing that creates it is
The rest is up to you reader of the unreadable

Epilogue: If anyone believes they may have found the key please see the FAQ

a) What's in it for me?
b) How do I delete the answer I thought correct but which could influence the outcome of the war?
c) Is there really belief different from habit?
d) How do I challenge the lack of authority
e) What are you doing tonight
f) Why is there no author
g) How will I ensure my family will be safe
h) What do I do if I put my prescription in the ignition
i) Who do you think you are

Mosquito Hologram /

Sleep is a tree with a thousand rivers
CRISPR mutant mosquitoes you can bet
Are weaponized former people who neither
Sleep nor eat but happily work and don't need
To be destroyed for quite some time

The energy flowing torqued through dying
Suffering hatred joy release
Ecstasy really if you jump up

Do your feet land on the ground
Or do you splash into water in the sleep of the moment
Is the moment of awareness
Maybe every word
A fleeting place marker in that slow wave

Sleep not tethered to the dock
Sleep with one eye open flying over the network of rivers
Sleep after sex in a wave
Of mosquitoes of your former selves

The way light falls on a two-dimensional interference pattern

Pi /

Suppose a circle suppose a point
The point at which caring overcomes you
The point at which flames catch fire
Suppose a Feynman diagram of your
Relationship to a god suppose rose-
Breasted grosbeaks the rich songs
Of both sexes the point at which the mind
Or some part of its action becomes a circle
You have to ask yourself if the circles
Get progressively smaller or larger
Now that you have this prison suppose
A circle suppose a temenos whose centre
Is notwithstanding trichobothria pulling
Ancient motion into present hearing
A loop as one of your pasts begins to
Encroach why is sacred space
Empty but for a few things model
Airplanes juneberry the Guelph
Formation wavelengths of ultraviolet
Missed phone calls that left no messages
Amuse-oreilles

Ambush Loop with Hidden Processes /

Bursting dreaming rabid light
Biting into the forest clearing but
What if
One of these flash occurrences
Could save your life nightfall seaswell
Of meadowgrass for instance also a burst
I am always immersed in
The before before
I go to Sunday School with the gift-
Sized new nearly pocket bible
With a zipper before the test before the kiss
Before the olive grey sky of
The horizon sweeps across the lake
And drowns our Flying Dutchman
Before I pick up the phone to call
Emmanuel who says our reason insists on these things
Though the world may not resemble
Our thinking in the least and feeling
Has the purpose of guiding
Every word a receptor a pair of glasses a pair
Of dice aperitif remember
It could appear anywhere along the continuum
Of a season
That flashes only a small house of viewing and could be
Hazardous a misdirection please
Waken safely every inside
Its own outside for which we have
No containment techniques

Every object the outside
Of a subject and within every subject
Another object dreaming

Equilibrium Vector /

A miniature rocket may be launched from the hat of a passerby   a purchase may be triggered   gravity privatized   a boy witness a Canadair Sabre slice into the embrace of a lake   a sleeper awaken

Small llamas   small lamentations   a cynic surrender a narrow aptitude for love   small emendations   small emus

I used to believe heaven inhabited a handful of sand   but that's a Fermi estimation   an unverifiable estimate   but well so what   it's not what I left on the subway   the memorial of sand is glass and sure enough it was not at the lost and found and I am filled with curiosity   what should I say   decollecting may begin at any time

And your proposals may save the lives of millions   or just make you more at home allowing the punished to be punished further   before I walk out into the woods   and the blood root

First shone its light   when I couldn't remember what I was   slip of feather through breeze   door for nightwords   that crashed into a deer or   that danced with wasps on a building site   fondled   dreamed later with fear   squall-swept decks of sailboats   hemorrhage drowner

The mortar that never exploded   thudding into earth at my father's wrist   driver of the Jeep killed   what really could have changed   changed really what   what had   what have   what is   the inwardness of stone   sky crushed with ice in the river   the grey owl suddenly appearing with a snap of her head   and so when I answered the door   I was surprised to find it was me who'd been knocking all this time

Sinthomes of Distributed Clairvoyance /

Note in a safety deposit box at the Hauptbahnhof
Time doesn't know me in books of sand blight-
Irrigation trumpet-calendar black-throated
Blue at the base of the window of sky slice
Of life recovering from its collision breathing bag
As children we'd suck out the skulls of tiny insects
To get at their song specimens but the
Evidence for this is inconveniently sketchy
Milne using an oil brush for watercolour
An apprentice to darkness for a while
Will take on the appearance of light porosity
Where a surface is bigger than any memory
And in fact absorbs your glance wherever it goes
And that muteness is what used to be called
The looking back of the thing you're looking at
As if it could actually be unlocked

Life Line /

I've been walking through fields of fireweed for quite some time
Ghost seeds drifting along the edges of transparency etching now
right to the forest of larch and maple
Things seem closer once you can say their names yet some of the
most important things we've believed in together remain unsaid
shadows are
Transparent and the red-shafted flicker I've never seen in the
politics of fear
Fear our failure can be burnt off with nitrogen someone once said
when the sun sets
Things don't vanish so much as forget themselves

What is a walk though this meadow but a walk through this meadow
Yellow-shafted flicker fireweed ghosts goldenrod
Sweetgrass milkweed ghosts wind
About twelve degrees Celsius where some deer rested the dead
Tried to farm this meadow and found a library of stones

The Temperature of Noise /

> *Light turns out to be only noise.*
> —Arkadii Dragomoshchenko

Noise is the wilderness of heaven
A flying robot the size of a mosquito

You might hear the mosquito with your radar pin
But you don't know who said it

I'm just walking out along the edge of that conversation now
And can't hear anything but fluorescent moonlight
Slipping over everything studying sharpening
Obliterating longing

Elision over the boundaries
The boundarylessness of the noise

Of the voice in the jar of wood frog politics of family of traffic of lichen
Shooting star tracheal buzzsaw belligerence along the road clearance bombardment
Rubble cries ropes of moonlight

I'm leaning toward an atomic theory of mental life
An atomic theory of breathing
The one with the swerve in it
But not far enough

So many swerves the amplitudes of years
But it's a big room

We are finally sitting alone in it
With a painting by Munch and one by Monkman
And one that you did a long time ago or was that mine
Or is that the windows

What's happening with the temperature of light on the wall
Is that my memory furniture
Foundering through bird calls traffic accidents finger pointing
The line squalls the lit motes the echoes

Through the sound waves divers' flares

Escape Oracle /

Each word a pelican
Who folds up and dives
Into the current of your brain

What is the nature of a message
Given a single word's origami

What if each syllable were an escape oracle
And every moment a locked drawer

What if I'm floating on the raft of an archaic vowel I don't know how to form

What if I'm in the garden of splendour
And the raven is quicker

Each self is a folded thing

The moment I could have looked back
The moment I could have spoken

Think with the knowing of falling I need to remind myself

Words are awing

Living is diving

It Matters /

That the thinking of the forest is not my thinking
That things learned to fly by manipulating the airwaves
That those who love deepest have cellos for hearts
That those who love deepest have ouds for hearts
That those who love deepest have mbiras for hearts
That those who love deepest have kotos for hearts
That those who love deepest have dewe'iganag for hearts

It matters
That things have plans of their own
That water flows uphill in dreams
That words are your breath
Wrapped in the music of each of your histories
That time opens its profligate book

It matters
That I'm an animal made of animals
That the interior of things is farther away than I can imagine
That in winter sun liquid silver drips off the roof
That delta gamma omicron
That the yet to come is already here

It matters
That language is a manipulated field recording
That to many I may not even appear as a being
Especially amongst the extinctions
That thirst is waves of someplace else
That you can only begin when you've already begun

That time is music
That zoom zaum Ursprache
We carry just happily here still

Capillaries of Sleep /

1) Slow wave

Rigged with snow-pocked streaked meteorites
Reading stations are established throughout the perimeter of the sentence

A magnification device allows a close look at late Q aggregates
Sweeping down the rock shelves into the bay

Sun beating the bushes with her stick of light

You're following shadow-maps sidewise into current-shear

2) The nature of porosity

Confess it's you drifting through walls mesh
Of electromagnetic fields

Your being here an asymptote

You smell like wind carried off the tops of breakers or through cedar underbrush

You conscript methylation
The blood-brain barrier means nothing to you

You cross into words a vaccine for meaning like the picture of a loved one

And beauty falls everywhere around like snow interest rates radiation

The imaginary construct of what belongs to us

3) Wilderness making

Don't jump to conclusions though

Parliament is not in session
And it's hard to tell the petrotoxins from the corporate green
Wind debacles purifying violence
Is a way away not a house you can move into immediately not
A thought control experiment believe me
I'd like to have the answer
To your question you can't wave away
But there are no special destinies

Only something sky-like floating on the river

Only the namelessness of luck
Its tributaries and unnamed creatures

Any one of whom may be about to speak

Fossils of Experience Found in Human Anatomy /

A word a whirled a smeared
An ammonite hammer music
A whole childhood

A slice angle telescope
A hallucigenia wavelength keyhole
What the hearthook would still look for

Spirit glove hammer fin
A dreamwing aerial
Swiss army knife of touch caress finesse signal

A petal flame-coloured nautiloid wordhouse
Where each room still burns a different time

A purple bud puff
Adder quill
Fat straw Amazon's handgun

Ukiyo-e cattleya locket kalimba
A viola da gamba inkwell orchestra
Ah ah ah tree

Of smoke beehive ballot box a nutcase shell game in the
Nothing chrysanthemum peony monkshood exploding
Finely etched blooms

Red fig red phone red
Bat in a cave soap opera land mine kite
Some little red book alarm clock of the hologram of happiness

Losing Sleep /

That ocean that quotient that anaphora theatre
That patient that oh shhh can you hear it that one
Reanimating solar tincture that orchid that ore that
Tipped canoe those frugally burnt bridges she put in her scrapbook
That sticker that knocking box that kick-boxer balancing
That web-footed wetland that cursive lip that ooh-la-la that changes
Everything that echo that ochre that killer whale sonata
That humming philosopher that last breath that breach
Keening or kiss that squeamish parliament of downloaded
Apparatchiks this spike of heron's hunger rope bridges swaying
Through the markets I write them scribble them they me in from there
That distance that long closed off space those orange smudged depths
Dreamed of lures they'll have shunted they do down from the imagine
To underthinking overlooking that lunge of river trivia majuscule
one day revelation

This Is a Photograph of You /

On the beach where the swash zone is
Luminous timecurves sliding alizarin saffron bittersweet ivory
Ghosted goldenrod cherry blossom polished and tarnished silver
up to your feet your back to the lightwaves lightwaves and
Wavelengths of the sea of the sunset of a fast squadron
Of black skimmers skimming wave tops

Wave tops you are looking into
The eye of the camera into me into the night I have turned my
back to
To look at you you almost shadow in shimmer head tipped
Slightly right holding your right elbow with your left hand
Legs apart part drift part sway part dance
Hair blown shimmer across your eyes shadowed
By the coming night

Where you've caught a timecurve in a gesture I love and draw
everything through
The eye of the needle of itself including our being here many times
many times before being is longing
And though nothing really belongs to us

You answer that
Just like this this this
Shimmering loop of world

Debt Algorithm of Nitric Acid Cloud Particles /

Not a northern streak of sky god nor
The trailing salvation metaphors
Not the advent of the Million Dollar Man
Nor the abandoned trike maroon with
Nostalgia so chemically wrong nor the
Recreational sex practices that could have
Led to our deaths nor the lost languages
Of the people of the river nor the economy
Running on speculative self-interest not at the foot
Of the ship's prow now plowed up Main Street
And wedged between the borrowed buildings
From whose eaves orioles used to suspend
Their futures nor among the shrunken human
Fruit shriked in the thorn orchard
Or those still tied to their chairs their
Ozone-hole haloes nor out along
The stratospheric fictitious data-streamers
Across the liquid mirror
Of night each paradise of last light lit
From below the horizon its
Own scar each loaned life
Its true gifted opalescence

Shedding

The song is the song is the song
The song is
The song song song
Song the scatter-hoarding
Of what
We cannot say
Motion
Without moving
The intimacy of stillness
Also song without words
Also belonging without bees
The song of someone's fingers along your spine
The many songs of the mockingbird
Each one so carefully learned
A rope bridge the sudden
River in the gorge below
Beckoning you is the song
Is a garden of imperceptible forces
The look the phoebe gave you from the railing
The quick glance backward
Yours or someone else's
The moment you'd sworn you'd never forget
The song is
A cloudburst of memory
The gorge calling you from the cliff in the rain
An inverted map of the underworld
A knife throwing its shimmervoice onto the ceiling in kitchen sunlight
The world throwing its shuttle into the momentary

Shed-shaped truth of you
The song the silence
It's leaving behind

Last Things /

This is where light comes to be itself
Where the angel of elision celebrates
Success a moment of veer
A point accumulates distance
Where sand is the memory of glass
And is what it is not sewing
Machines crocosmia machinations
Weather children wheatear VCR
Lionel Barrymore movies Swiss chard
Duct tape parachute drifters
Last dance chance
Saloons and the idea of fire
Requires the person's whole attention and motion
Is where things stop

How to Reimagine Some (but by No Means All) of the Impossible Foregoing Things /

Is (page 7)
"Irish Lake": A small spring-fed lake in what was Artemesia Township, now in Grey Highlands, Ontario, just north of Priceville (see below).

Shadow Water Radio (page 8)
"Proton Station...hacking treaties": These places/events are located in what was once called the Queen's Bush (and what once *was* forest) in Southern Ontario. With regard to Priceville in particular: In the early nineteenth century the vast "unsettled" area between Waterloo County, Lake Huron, and Georgian Bay—which in 1850 was divided into counties and townships (the first census was in 1851)—was of course Anishinaabe territory (and still is). The first contested treaty of 1836 was quickly followed by others until 1857—and even 1874 on the Peninsula. Settlers, mostly of Scottish and Irish origin had already begun infiltrating the area by the 1820s. Of the settlers, it's interesting that more than one thousand five hundred free and formerly enslaved Blacks pioneered scattered farms here. Many settled along the Peel and Wellesley Township border, with Glen Allan, Hawkesville, and Wallenstein as important centers. By the late 1840s some had made it up to what is now Durham and Priceville. When the government ordered the district surveyed many of the settlers could not afford to purchase the land they had laboured to clear. By the late 1850s migration out of the Queen's Bush had begun. Today African Canadians whose ancestors pioneered the Queen's Bush are represented in communities across Ontario. (https://www.heritagetrust.on.ca/en/plaques/the-queens-bush-settlement-1820–1867)

Despite the myth it appears that the settlement of Priceville was in fact named after a government land agent.

With regard to the treaties: Stephanie McMullen's unpublished MA thesis, *Disunity and Dispossession: Nawash Ojibwa and Potawatomi in the Saugeen Territory, 1836–1865*, details their fraught and sadly typical history of continued and incessant settler encroachment.

"Gene driver": "Like wormholes, gene drives are super-fast ways to get where you're going, they just warp evolution instead of space-time. The concept behind a gene drive is deceptively simple; it just means that a gene is passed down to offspring—and, therefore, spreads through a population—more than standard genetics would predict. If we could piggyback some useful trait onto a gene drive, we could manage entire populations on the genetic level, and much faster than classical selection." (http://epigenie.com/gene-drives-wormholes-of-biology/)

"Shimmering silence of the drive" is a phrase from Timothy Morton's essay "Buddhaphobia; Nothingness and the Fear of Things" in *Nothing: Three Inquiries in Buddhism*, but in this case applies to Freud's death drive, which he first called the "nirvana principle".

Soul Bodies (page 11)
"The who of things": Guimarães Rosa's phrase found in *Cannibal Metaphysics*, a transformative read written by Edwardo Viveiros de Castro and translated by Peter Skafish.

Dictionary of Overlapping Things (page 16)
"Thoughts like trains departing": The now famous experiments of Benjamin Libet have shown that there is a missing half second

between the onset of neural activity in the brain and our conscious perception of the event. Occurring in the brain but outside consciousness, as Brian Massumi writes in *Parables for the Virtual*. No one quite knows what goes on there; a half second is a very long time neurologically, but "Libet determined that thought covers up its lag: the awareness is 'backdated' so that each thought experiences itself to have been at the precise time the stimulus was applied." Not only that but a sensation that takes a half second to be felt can be modified by one that follows a quarter of second later. In perception time is recursive and loops back on itself, and "every first-time perception ... is already, virtually, a memory." A déjà vu.

"Kirlian photograph": Named after Russian electrician Semyon Davidovich Kirlian, Kirlian photography was discovered by accident. Semyon and his wife Valentina began studying and developing this high-voltage electrophotography in 1939. Kirlian photography became publicized in the 1970s by Sheila Ostrander and Lynn Schroeder in their book titled *Psychic Discoveries Behind the Iron Curtain*. The process doesn't require a camera. A sheet of photographic film is placed on top of a metal plate. Then, the object that is to be photographed is placed on top of the film. To create the initial exposure, high voltage current is applied to the metal plate. The electrical coronal discharge between the object and the metal plate is captured on the film. The high-voltage frequency applied to the metal plate rips the electrons from the atoms. Air around the photographed object becomes ionized. If that air contains any water, the resulting image will show the glowing silhouette and streamers around the object, which scientists call a "corona plasma discharge." Oils, sweat, bacteria, and other ionizing contaminants found on living tissues can also affect the resulting images.

Ravens Carry on their Research into Human Thinking (page 19)
"Dubious spindles, waved goblets, left-handed jewel boxes" are sea shells.

"Veronique" is the main character in Kieslowski's haunted and haunting 1991 film *The Double Life of Veronique*.

The One about the Nongivenness of Things ... (page 21)
"Wildernessing": See this post, "Wilderness Ontology" by Levi Bryant: https://larvalsubjects.wordpress.com/2017/08/31/wilderness-ontology-2/#more-8847

Vacuum Glass History (page 25)
"Flying skeletons": Pauguk (the Flying Skeleton) is from Ojibwe tradition, a detail I gleaned from *The Manitous: The Spiritual World of the Ojibway*, by Basil Johnston.

Light (page 27)
"The body is the true ghost": In *Cannibal Metaphysics* de Castro attempts to show how Amazonian peoples see that bodies are interchangeable and malleable. What knowledge is, is finding the person, that brightness, in the various, perhaps even fiery bodies.

Zeno's Attractor (page 28)
Such a thing didn't exist until now. However there have been attractors that are sets of values toward which dynamic systems tend but at which they never actually arrive for some time. Strange attractors are very sensitive to initial conditions and therefore partake of chaotic processes. As for Zeno, his paradoxes have been around for quite some time, though I've never seen his arrow or his heap of sand.

User's Manual (page 29)
"Edge cluster": "Inference of new biological knowledge, e.g., prediction of protein function, from protein-protein interaction (PPI) networks has received attention in the post-genomic era. A popular strategy has been to cluster the network into functionally coherent groups of proteins and predict protein function from the clusters. Traditionally, network research has focused on clustering of nodes. However, why favor nodes over edges, when clustering of edges may be preferred? For example, nodes belong to multiple functional groups, but clustering of nodes typically cannot capture the group overlap, while clustering of edges can. Clustering of adjacent edges that share many neighbors was proposed recently, outperforming different node clustering methods. However, since some biological processes can have characteristic 'signatures' throughout the network, not just locally, it may be of interest to consider edges that are not necessarily adjacent." (Solava, Michaels, Milenkovic, *Identifying edge clusters in networks via edge graphlet degree vectors (edge-GDVs) and edge-GDV-similarities*, Abstract) Non-local connections through non-adjacent edges. I'm taking the bus there now.

"Polyploidy": "Polyploidy is the heritable condition of possessing more than two complete sets of chromosomes... At first sight, the epigenetic changes observed in polyploids would seem to be deleterious because of their disruptive effects on regulatory patterns established by selection. However, these epigenetic changes might instead increase diversity and plasticity by allowing for rapid adaptation in polyploids." (http://www.nature.com/scitable/topicpage/polyploidy-1552814) Oh to be a polyploid.

Mereology (page 32)
After Donna J. Haraway, *Staying with the Trouble: Making Kin in the Chthulucene.*

"The South Atlantic Anomaly": (SAA) "An area where the Earth's inner Van Allen radiation belt comes closest to the Earth's surface, dipping down to an altitude of 200 kilometres (120 mi). This leads to an increased flux of energetic particles in this region and exposes orbiting satellites to higher-than-usual levels of radiation." (https://en.wikipedia.org/wiki/South_Atlantic_Anomaly)

"Without the protection of the Earth's atmosphere, cosmonauts were exposed to higher levels of radiation from a steady flux of cosmic rays and trapped protons from the South Atlantic Anomaly. [The] daily dose is approximately that received from natural background radiation on Earth in two years." (https://en.wikipedia.org/wiki/Mir#Accidents)

"Meera Bai": a celebrated early 16th century Hindu mystic poet who became revered as a saint in the Bhakti movement.

"Mountain Lifter" is one of her names for Krishna.

Collection (page 37)
"How to bend time": In particle physics there are many things beyond our ken, and certainly my ken with my hopeless mathematics. A light cone links past and future through an event with photons, but gravity and chaos also impinge on this nifty model allowing, in string theory, such even neater things as the time reversal and "spooky action at a distance" (Einstein) under entanglement. Dream can be seen as a spacelike vector; déjà vu a time-like vector.

But the key is that time is emergent with the event and in overtaking other events can be bent. Compare Libet's missing half second. Hmm.

"Laganology": No such word I'm afraid. However, if *jetsam*, in maritime law, is what is thrown overboard to lighten a ship in distress and is wreckage that washes on shore, *lagan* is marine debris lying on the ocean bed (sometimes marked with a buoy) that can be recovered (salvaged). *Laganology* might then be the bringing to the surface the stories of how these things got there, or perhaps the study of the things themselves, or the methods of recovery.

Unidentified Poetic Object (page 38)
"Pyrotechnical blowgun": A weapon taken from the arsenal of Tamas Dobozy in his wonderful book of linked short stories, *Siege 13*.

Pallasite (page 39)
"Pallasites are the most beautiful of all meteorites. They are stony-iron meteorites derived from an extinct planet that was destroyed during the formation of our solar system (approximately 4.5 billion years ago). They come from the boundary between the silica rich mantle and the iron-nickel core of the planet and were torn away from the planet by a catastrophic impact with another planet or asteroid. Pallasites contain olivine (Peridot) 'space gems' embedded in an iron nickel matrix. When sliced thinly and polished, the stable pallasites make exceptional display pieces reminiscent of a stained-glass window in a Church!" (http://www.arizonaskiesmeteorites.com/AZ_Skies_Links/Stony_Irons/)

In the Field (page 41)
"Phytochrome": A photoreceptor in plants responsible for a plant's sensing of both far-red and red light. Far-red is the last light a plant senses in the evening and red is the first. In this way perhaps surprisingly, the plant measures the length of continuous darkness in order to optimize its growth and flowering. See Daniel Chamovitz, *What a Plant Knows: A Field Guide to the Senses*, for this and other fascinating stuff such as how a Venus flytrap knows when to snap shut.

"Bottle cap foam dart marble Donald Duck Pez dispenser orange glass shard": This great list of crow gifts is culled from Jennifer Ackerman, *The Genius of Birds*.

"Kettle": "Kame and kettle topography is an indicator of a high-discharge supraglacial and englacial drainage system of a glacier in the final stages of melt, and large quantities of glacially derived debris associated with meltwater." (http://link.springer.com/referenceworkentry/10.1007%2F978-90-481-2642-2_312)

Interregnum of Extractions (page 44)
"Hit a circle four inches square": William Burroughs.

Apantomancy (page 46)
Divination through the use of whatever happens to be at hand.

"N+1": The opposite of "decollecting" (in *The Truth I Swear* and *Equilibrium Vector*). Some of the object discourse in the book reflects the work of Peter Schwenger in his compelling *The Tears of Things: Melancholy and Physical Objects*, for instance: "Everything outside of the categories by which we allow ourselves to see the real is categorized ... as a merely seeming reality—that is as hallucination. But a book like the *Codex Seraphinianus* reminds us that categories themselves, with their claims to reflect the real, may be the most delusory hallucination of all." And quoting Baudrillard, "the metamorphoses, the ruses, the strategies of the object surpasses the subject's understanding."

Varves (page 47)
"Graptolites": Literally stone writing, but writing written by colonies of tiny animals that shared the same skeletal letter. They lived in the Upper Cambrian to the Lower Carboniferous and the writing is fossiliferous.

The Visitors (page 48)
"Davis' Vegetable Pain Killer": Common over-the-counter remedy in the nineteenth century. The "vegetable" was a patented (1845) recipe that included opium. We found an intact hand-blown glass bottle—alas empty—in a midden on our property.

How to Survive a Decomposition Event (page 50)
"The wind puts its mouth to ...": "The storm puts its mouth to the house ... It sets its mouth to our soul/and blows...." ("A Winter Night," Tomas Tranströmer, translated by Robin Fulton)

Cloud Encounter Box with Flow-Through Lungs (page 53)
"Pyrodictium, stella, haloarcula": Haloarcula and pyrodictium are archaea rather than bacteria and are extremophiles (!); they can take on a range of shapes and environments including, for some, those loaded with heavy metals and so may be the future models for life on what remains of earth. Stella are a flat rather than the typical cylindrical bacteria, but not much has been explored about

them since a couple of USSR articles published in the '70s and '80s, so perhaps they don't really exist.

Tangut Cloud Crumhorn (page 56)
"The black city": Kara-Khoto (Etzina), a once thriving Tangut centre in Inner Mongolia (Western Xia) from 1032 to approximately 1372.

Imaginary Berlin (page 58)
Tropes from Wim Wenders' 1987 film *Wings of Desire* provide a setting for the exploration of a couple of unique manuscripts, one, known as the Voynich Manuscript, dating from the early fifteenth century which, though having similarities with herbals, zodiacal, and alchemical texts of the time and though displaying elements of natural languages we know or encrypted code texts, remains undeciphered. (See http://www.voynich.nu/index.html and https://www.jasondavies.com/voynich/#outside_front_cover/0.398/0.247/2.00) The other is the *Codex Seraphinianus*, an encyclopedia of an imaginary world (https://www.wired.com/2013/10/codex-seraphinianus-interview/) created by architect and industrial designer-turned-artist Luigi Serafini and published in 1981 that also features a unique and indecipherable writing system.

"Schreibtischtäter": Deskman, bureaucrat, pencil pusher; someone working behind the scenes, like the mastermind of a crime. Here however, perhaps angel, or only the writer. The term has also been used in a more sinister fashion, as "desk murderer," referring specifically to Nazi bureaucrats of the Holocaust. The angels in the Wenders film are the opposite of murderers; they're actually "caring" bureaucrats (but it is a question in the film).

"Bsafe": Pencilled cryptically on one of the opening leaves of the Voynich manuscript.

"Hidden Markov Model": "One in which you observe a sequence of emissions, but do not know the sequence of states the model went through to generate the emissions. Analyses of hidden Markov models seek to recover the sequence of states from the observed data." (https://www.mathworks.com/help/stats/hidden-markov-models-hmm.html?s_tid=gn_loc_drop)

Mosquito Hologram (page 65)
"CRISPR": A family of DNA sequences in bacteria. The sequences contain snippets of DNA from viruses that have attacked the bacterium. These snippets are used by the bacterium to detect and destroy DNA from further attacks by similar viruses. These sequences play a key role in a bacterial defense system, and form the basis of a genome editing technology known as CRISPR/Cas9 that allows permanent modification of genes within organisms. (https://en.wikipedia.org/wiki/CRISPR)

Pi (page 66)
"Trichobothria": "Trichobothria (singular trichobothrium) are elongate setae ('hairs') present in arachnids, various orders of insects, and myriapods that function in the detection of airborne vibrations and currents. In 1883 Friedrich Dahl observed that they were deflected by the sound waves from a violin and labelled them 'hearing hairs.'" (https://en.wikipedia.org/wiki/Trichobothria)

Ambush Loop with Hidden Processes (page 67)
"Flying Dutchman": Not a ghost ship, nor an opera, though that particular day was certainly dramatic; we managed to avoid

becoming ghosts ourselves. We were sailing an FD (for short): a twenty-foot one-design high-performance two-person monohull racing dinghy, developed in the early 1950s in the Netherlands (according to Wikipedia) that belonged to my friend John Draper in an international racing series hosted by the Oakville Yacht Club when the fleet got clobbered by a very serious line squall. We were planing downwind on jib alone and could hardly see ten feet through the wind-driven rain as all kinds of nightmare floating debris from other boats—life jackets, paddles—appeared in the heavy seas and vanished in our wake. We were the youngest crew in the event.

Sinthomes of Distributed Clairvoyance (page 71)
"Sinthome": "In his seminar 'L'angoisse' (1962–63) [Lacan] states that the symptom does not call for interpretation: in itself it is not a call to the Other but a pure jouissance addressed to no one. This is a shift from the linguistic definition of the symptom—as a signifier—to his assertion that 'the symptom can only be defined as the way in which each subject enjoys (*jouit*) the unconscious in so far as the unconscious determines the subject.' He goes from conceiving the symptom as a message which can be deciphered by reference to the unconscious structured like a language to seeing it as the trace of the particular modality of the subject's *jouissance*." (https://en.wikipedia.org/wiki/Sinthome)

And: "The sinthome does not present an available language to be decoded..." (Eric Cazdyn, "Enlightenment, Revolution, Cure: The Problem of Praxis and the Radical Nothingness of the Future" in *Nothing: Three Inquiries in Buddhism*)

"Darkness ... will take on the appearance of light": A glancing derivative from "Pyrrho: ... The right eye must not trust the left eye, and for some time light must be called darkness: this is the path that you must tread. Do not imagine that it will lead you to fruit trees and fair pastures.... The Elder: Ah, friend! Silence and laughter is that now your whole philosophy? Pyrrho: There might be a worse." (Nietzsche, *The Wanderer and His Shadow*, which I first found at the Synthetic Zero website: https//syntheticzero.net)

It Matters (page 76)
"Dewe'iganag": Ojibwe hand drums.

"Zaum": The name the Russian Futurists Aleksei Kruchenykh and Velimir Khlebnikov gave to their explorations in transrational sonic language creation in 1913.

"Ursprache": German, meaning original or proto-language and one of the foci of Hugo Ball and Dadaism in its attempts to recover the original language in which humans, gods, and creatures could communicate. (And just at proofing I found this fascinating article on the related theory of ideophones: https://aeon.co/essays/in-the-beginning-was-the-word-and-the-word-was-embodied?utm_source=Aeon+Newsletter.)

Capillaries of Sleep (page 78)
"Q aggregates": Financial calculations applying Tobin's q in aggregate to markets showing the ratio of the value of a stock market as a whole to net assets at replacement cost.

"Methylation": "DNA methylation is an epigenetic mechanism that occurs by the addition of a methyl group to DNA, thereby often modifying the function of the genes and affecting gene expression." (https://www.whatisepigenetics.com/dna-methylation/)

Some of these changes could also be inheritable.

Fossils of Experience Found in Human Anatomy (page 80)
"Tree of smoke": "... a shadowy realm where ideology and intelligence, disinformation and revelation overlap ... [a] system of epistemological nihilism created by various rival factions in the intelligence community." (Jackson Lears, "What We Don't Talk about When We Talk about Russian Hacking," LRB Vol.40 #1, 4 Jan 2018, quoting novelist Denis Johnson's term)

This Is a Photograph of You (page 82)
"Timecurve": Properly, *time curve.* "A general approach to [visualizing] patterns of evolution in temporal data, such as: progression and stagnation, sudden changes, regularity and irregularity, reversals to previous states.... Time curves are based on the metaphor of folding a timeline visualization into itself so as to bring similar time points close to each other." (http://www.aviz.fr/~bbach/timecurves/)

There's also a fabulous piece of minimalist piano music by William Duckworth called *The Time Curve Preludes.*

Last Things (page 86)
"Last dance chance": Nod to Meredith Monk's "Last Song" from her 2008 *Impermanence* album.

Acknowledgements /

"Light" is for Sean; "Excommunicados," "Unfolding," "This Is a Photograph of You" for Charlene.

Thanks to the editors of the following venues who first published (sometimes in different guises) some of the pieces in this book: *Filling Station* ("User's Manual," "The Truth I Swear"); *The New Quarterly* (quite some time ago a version of "Lightheadedness" appeared in its pages); *Prairie Fire* ("Collection / How to Bend Time with a Flashlight in Your Own Home"); *Rampike* ("Dictionary of Overlapping Things," "Fizzed"); *Literary Review of Canada* ("Varves / How to Repair an Atomic Clock with Graptolites"); *Vallum* ("The Incommensurate," which won second prize in its 2016 poetry contest and appeared in the spring 2017 issue.); *Dusie* ("Words"); Harvey Hix's *In Quire* blog in the Crawford project ("It Matters"); and the 2018 League of Canadian Poets' fundraising anthology about trees and the environment, *Heartwood: Poems for the Love of Trees* ("Marks").

Thanks to Naomi Norquay of the Old Durham Road Cemetery Committee, to Stephanie McMullen for sharing her thesis on the Saugeen Treaties, to Sharon Mohr, Ashley O'Brien, Jen Base, Vita and Jeff Wind, Carole Kowalchuk, Richard Henderson and Marion Meyers for playing the cover game, to Loris Lesynski for "amuse-oreilles" and much more, to Maureen Harris for her sharp eye, to Gary Barwin, Jeanette Lynes, and Edward Carson for their generosity, to my editor Helen Guri for her insightful interventions, to Alayna Munce for the fine fine tuning, to Marijke Friesen for her creative visual insight and flexibility, and to Barry Dempster and Kitty because. And to my wife, Charlene Winger, especially and always.

BRIAN HENDERSON has been a Governor General's Award finalist and a finalist for the CAA Chalmers Award for Poetry. He is the author of eleven previous volumes of poetry.